The Refuge

Donald E Waller Jr

TABLE OF CONTENTS

Copyright 3

Introduction 5

Welcome 6

Taxi Cab Ministry 7

Nursing Home Ministry 13

Massage Ministry 24

Miracles 32

Principles to Live by 36

About the Author 71

COPYRIGHT

Warner Faith
Hatchette Book Group USA
1271 Avenue of the Americas, New York, NY10020

Visit our Website at www.faithwords.com

Printed in the United States of America
First Edition: October 2006
10 9 8 7 6 5 4 3 2 1
ISBN-13: 978-0-446-57827-1
ISBN-10:0-446-57827-4
LCCN: 2006928321

The Refuge

ISBN 979-888831019-9

US $0.99
50099

9 798888 310199

INTRODUCTION

The center of our belief system needs to come from the core of our being, from beginning of life to the end. the righteousness (meaning and understanding of a right relationship with our Living God) Finding the provision of the Blood poured out on Calvary brings a complete refuge in Jesus Christ our Savior and Lord, and security through the end of time. Psalm 14:2

WELCOME

My name is Donald E Waller Jr. This book is about sharing the stories of my life and ministry. Through the years I've had many opportunities to reach out to many people sharing the love of Jesus in word and deed. It is inspirational ministry stories about people who have personal and life changing encounters with Jesus. It includes miracles I have seen and experienced, as well as basic foundations for living a Christian life. Jesus is The Refuge.

TAXI CAB MINISTRY

The first chapter contains stories about my time as a taxi cab driver. It was a blessing to see people open their hearts about their life experiences. That made it possible for me to point them to Christ as the way, the truth, and the life.

The first story I would like to share is about a very intoxicated lady that I picked up at a local nightclub. When we got to the motel she kept passing out, but I aroused her enough to get her to walk and help me get her to her room. I helped her get to the bed and left.

About two weeks later she called for another ride to town. She said I looked familiar and even asked if we had met before. I told her that we had and that I was the taxi driver that took her home from the nightclub two weeks ago. I told her how concerned I was for her and that she should not get drunk again because she could get hurt.

I told her that Jesus loved her that he wanted to come into her heart and cleanse her from all of the things she had done in her past.   She began weeping and crying and said, "I know my mother and dad didn't want me to leave home, but I did anyway. I have been doing some wrong things and running from God, but I know you're right. You're a confirmation for me to do what I need to do. I need to go home, read my Bible, get back in church and do the right thing. I need to get a career that I can do. Thank you so much for bringing me home the other night and making sure I was all right. I am calling my mom and dad right now and telling them I'm coming home. Thank you so much and hope to see you again either here or when we get to heaven."

The next story is about a man who was a taxi driver but had to quit because of his alcohol addiction. We were good friends and enjoyed talking about fishing and hunting. Once in a while he would buy cruise time in the taxi, and we would just ride around for hours. Many times, I would encourage him to get some help, and I knew just the one to help him. I would tell him that God Almighty is able to help and deliver him from his drinking. I told him how God could save his soul and give him a new life in Christ.

One day he wanted me to take him to the lake. As we sat there and visited, I shared the gospel with him that Jesus was the one that can heal, deliver and set him free from the drinking and give him a new life that day in my taxi. He accepted Jesus Christ as his personal savior and was immediately cleansed and set free. He had a new home in heaven, a new heart and freedom from his drinking.

Following this miracle, he lived another six months. I was able to minister to his family at the funeral and also lead them to Christ. They were shocked when they learned all that he had been going through. It was wonderful to be able to tell them that he's with Jesus now and they can see him again someday. The family was greatly blessed and encouraged. I was humbly blessed that I was able to minister to them that day and see souls added to the Kingdom of God. What a day that was! It was a glorious day in that Funeral home.

The next story is about a little baby. One day I was coming in after a taxi run and when I looked up, I saw a baby crawling in the street. I stopped the car and rushed over to get the baby. I went from house to house until I found the mother. I admonished her about how close her baby came to being killed. I also assured her that if she didn't keep track of her baby at all times, I would be forced to turn her in to the authorities. I also told her I was pretty shaken up about finding the baby in the middle of the street and could easily have run over the baby if I hadn't been watching closely while I was driving. After I settled down a little bit, I reached out to the mom and prayed for her. I gave her my name and told her to call if she needed help and I would come. Every time I went by that part of town I would drive past to see if the baby was ok. Sometimes the baby would be dressed and playing in the yard, but she was never in the street again.

My next story is all about a lady who became a special friend. She didn't have a vehicle, so she rode a taxi several times a week. People could ask for a specific driver to pick them up and that is what she did. I got to know her and her five children. Her husband, who traveled a lot because of his job, was only home once or twice a month. The children were teenagers, so she had a big responsibility taking care of them. She became very passionate for the elderly, so she visited the nursing facilities and encouraged those folks. She was a Christian lady, but suffered from depression and fear. My wife met her, and they became close friends. She went to church with us and we shared the word of God as well as ministry opportunities in the kingdom of God together. As we progressed in relationship with her and her children, we began to share with them and encourage them and they began to come to church. We had the opportunity to baptize the children and see them grow up in the Lord. She continued to grow in her relationship with Jesus and the doubt and fear and the depression was lifted off her. It was a blessing to see her become closer to Jesus every day. She had a great compassion for people and became very instrumental in reaching out to others. She had many struggles in life but she overcame them all because she knew that there's nothing impossible with God. This faith was tested when one of her daughters was involved in a serious car accident and was paralyzed for quite a while. God did a miracle, and she was able to walk again. God is so faithful!

Philippians 4:13 says, "I can do all things through Christ who gives me strength." The word of God is true and if you will meditate on the word of God and reach out to him, he will meet your needs. In Jeremiah 32:17b it says that nothing is too hard for God. Luke 1:37 says nothing is impossible with God. God can do a miracle in your life if you will believe him for it. Psalms chapter 1 tells us to meditate on the word of God day and night. I am encouraging you to read the word of God and get a hold of the principles that I'm sharing. It will feed your soul and encourage you. If you're not going to church, it is essential to find a local church, so you can grow in Christ as you associate with other Christians. Rise up my friend and be encouraged to follow the Lord and let him minister to your heart. Be still and know that He is God.

I had another special friend during this taxicab ministry time. It encouraged me so much to see him set free that it put me on a new level of walk and trust in the Lord. He drank too much alcohol and had all kinds of problems. In John 14:6 Jesus said, "I am the way and the truth, and the life and no man comes to the father but by me." As I shared Jesus with him, he bowed his knee to the king of glory Jesus Christ and accepted Jesus as his personal savior and lord. He wept before God as he gave it all to him. The Holy Spirit revealed to this man that there was a better way than what he was doing. Jesus came into his heart and transformed him, set him free and everything was lifted off him. It was God's divine will that he be set free and be an instrument of the Holy Spirit to be used by God in his life. He committed himself to reading the word of God and doing everything that God wanted him to do. He rose up as a man of God and began to minister about Jesus everywhere he went. What happened to my friend can happen to you.

NURSING HOME MINISTRY

The next chapter talks about another phase of my life. I began working in nursing facilities and I had the opportunity to be trained and work as a physical therapy technician. The licensed physical therapist would set up the exercise program or walking program, and then I was allowed to work with the residents to help them exercise or walk. I was also allowed to pray with the residents and encourage them that Jesus still loved them. We had an exercise group, and I was able to get them to move their arms and legs. I had devotions and prayer time and shared the word of God daily. Those 15 years were very exciting with great opportunities to share the love of Jesus. God did many wonderful things.

The first story is about a lady that had been admitted to the nursing facility, and the doctor had given orders just to keep her comfortable until the end of her life. I begin to work with the maintenance of joint and muscle integrity to keep her comfortable. As I shared with her and prayed with her, she told me that she was not ready to just give up and die. It was her desire to live a while longer and to walk again. She asked if I would help her, and of course I said I would. I got permission from her doctor to begin, and we progressed the exercise by sitting on the side of the bed and then standing. Before long, she was able to stand beside a fixed rail in the facility. I encouraged her to stand for as long as she could tolerate. I also taught her breathing techniques and prayed for her and encouraged her every day. There were times when she was weak or hurting and then we would begin to pray and believe God to take one step at a time. She was finally able to take a short walk there in the facility. God answered our prayers, and she was able to enjoy her last days there in the nursing home. God gave her the desire of her heart to be able to walk again. It was a miracle and quite an experience to be there as God answered her prayers.

This next story is about a young woman who was a resident in the facilities. She had been in a terrible car accident. She couldn't talk and her legs and arms were all drawn up. According to the doctor she would be that way the rest of her life because of her condition. I began working with her just doing range of motion and a maintenance program. The Lord began to stir my heart that there was more that he wanted to do with her. I began to seek the orders that were required to work with her daily with range of motion. Even though she couldn't speak, I would talk to her. I kept speaking to her and encouraging her. I would call her by her name and tell her about the weather. I read the bible to her. During this time, I was able to visit with her family and encourage them not to give up hope. I continued talking to her and doing her exercises, but I didn't see much improvement.

I went to work on a Monday morning, and she wasn't there. I began to ask questions about where she had gone, and they wouldn't tell me. I couldn't find out anything except that the family had taken her somewhere. I just had to deal with it because nobody would tell me anything. I had to just take it to the Lord and leave it there. I never stopped praying for her. The old song says just take it to the Lord and leave it there. The whole song says to take your burdens to the Lord and leave it there because he's the only one that can fix it. Two years had passed since I had seen or heard anything about her. I had gone to massage school and was now a massage therapist working out of my home. One summer afternoon someone knocked on the door and there stood a beautiful young lady. I didn't recognize her right off, but she spoke her name and said she had been in the nursing facility where I was employed.   She reminded me how I had never stopped talking to her and never gave up on her. She was walking, talking and having a good life. She was completely healed, and I was so happy and blessed to see her.

I want to remind you that God is not done if he says he's not done. I want to encourage you to stand on the word of God no matter what because he never gives up, so we should never give up. God can and will do miracles today, if we will pray and believe.

I met another lady in a nursing facility who was blind, depressed, and very frail . She couldn't do anything and didn't want to try to do anything. She had lost her husband and was now up in years. I began to work with her and to encourage her and talk to her. I became her friend. Then I was able to get her to exercise and sit her up on the side of the bed. I talked to her about the Lord. She was very emotional all the time because she had been abused in her life. She had many problems that burdened her. I encouraged her to take those burdens to the Lord and leave them there. We began to pray and believe that God was going to do more in her life.

She began to make some progress and get in the wheelchair. Then I was able to get her out of her room a little bit and talk to her some more about the Lord and encourage her that everything was going to be alright. We had a little short service there in the facility and she said that she had a favorite song, "One Day At A Time." I wasn't familiar with it at the time, but as she sang it, I was able to play it by ear. When we sang her favorite song, she started coming out of it. I started getting her out of her room every day and singing her favorite song. It touched her heart and my heart, and she was much happier. Jesus began to bring her strength back and then she had more good days than bad ones. God was and is always so good.

The next story is about a lady whose frail body caused her to be depressed and in tremendous pain. As we became friends, she told me about the hard life she led. She and her husband had several children, but he became an alcoholic and did not provide for the family. Many times, she had to get the rifle and shoot a squirrel to make squirrel and dumplings to feed her family. By the time the children were grown; she was just tired and had lost her joy. I reminded her that Jesus loved her, and that she deserved to have some joy in her last days. She began to get in the wheelchair and come to the lobby to join us for singing and devotions. She started trying to walk and was able to take a few steps. It was a blessing to be a close friend and to be able to encourage her by reading the Bible and praying with her. There were lots of activities available for fun and fellowship with the other residents. One thing that I remember was a hat contest. It was so much fun to see her win the contest and have some happiness in her last days before she went home to be with the Lord.

This story is about a gentleman who had a museum in town. He was in the nursing facility because he had had a heart attack. He was very cantankerous and wasn't willing to cooperate with the nursing staff. He was always mean to the nurses and tried to hit them. They couldn't do anything with him so guess who got to do his baths and take care of him. I did! He had a very foul mouth, and it was a challenge to minister to him. I kept talking to him and telling him that God loves him. I kept working with him and praying for him. One day I pushed his wheelchair down to the lobby for singing and devotion time. I put his chair close to the piano. He wouldn't sing or talk or respond until I asked him what his favorite song was. He said it was "Living By Faith." I didn't know the song but was able to play it by ear. As he sang this song there was a breakthrough. God touched his hard heart, and he began to change. Hearing his favorite song reminded him of what Jesus had done. He stopped cursing and hitting the nurses. His last days in the nursing home were much different than his first days.

Another gentleman that had a stroke situation was very cantankerous and spoke harshly to others. He didn't want to walk or do anything but lay in bed. As I began to exercise him and talk to him, I told him he needed to get up and walk. I repeated this process every day and kept encouraging him until finally one day he said, "You're not gonna shut up until I get up and walk, are you?"

I said, "No sir, because I'm here to help you!" Starting that day, he began to sit up on the side of the bed and eventually gained the strength to stand up, exercise, and even walk. As we worked each day, he started getting motivated to get out and start associating with others. He began to clean up his language and participate in church services. It was great to see God come down and help him get back to living his life.

I met another gentleman who reacted in similar ways to his stroke that the previous man had. Although he was resistant, I began to build a friendship with him and found out that he and I had a friend in common. God gave us a breakthrough and then we found out that we had other friends in common. That bond of mutual friends allowed him to trust me and soon he began to walk and connect with life again. He began to come out of his shell and serve God with an open heart. God allowed me to continue to pray with him and see him delivered from past mistakes that had weighed him down. He was set free at last!

Another friend at the facility was a very sweet lady who consecrated her life to the Lord but still struggled with depression and fear. It was hard for her to even come out of her room. I began to encourage her and little by little I was able to get her to walk a bit. One day I told her we're having singing and devotion time and since she had served God all her life it was time to come again and glorify him. She didn't decide to come that day, but I kept working with her and until one day she came and sat by the piano. She asked me for a song, but since I didn't know it, I had to work on it. When I finally sang it to her, she lit up completely. She was so full of joy and happiness! God just came down through that song and touched her. She was set completely free and was down there every day we had singing and devotions. She was acting completely different because there was no more depression, no more doubt, no more fear! She lived the rest of her days happy in Jesus.

A remarkable lady that came into the facility was someone I will never forget. She was close to 100 years old, was very clear headed, and loved to talk. Her doctor ordered a specific diet designed to help her improve her health. On her first day, I went in to visit with her. As soon as I walked in she looked straight at me and said, "Sonny boy let me tell you something, I want you to go down there and tell the administrator that I want you to go to Hardee's right now and get me some biscuits and gravy. I have to have a little grease to get my food down every day. I've been eating this way for years and I'm not gonna stop now. You can tell the doctor what I said!"

I went down and told the administrator what the little lady had said. She sent me on my way to get the little lady her biscuits and gravy. As long as she ate the other things the doctor ordered, she got to eat her biscuits and gravy at least 3 times a week. She did walk again, and God blessed her with many good days for the rest of her life.

There was another friend in the nursing home who came after breaking her hip. She became so depressed that I couldn't get her to do anything. I just kept praying for her and trying to get her to exercise her body. She was full of fear that she might hurt herself. At her age, continuing to just lay in bed could do real damage to her health. I kept trying to convince her that the doctor's orders were designed to help her get better, and she must do her best to get up and walk. After much prayer and constant encouragement, she began to get up. Little by little she was able to progress to100 feet. Her confidence pushed her to go higher and praise God, she had a tremendous breakthrough!

There were many residents through the years who had breakthrough moments of joy being brought back into their lives. The interesting thing about joy is JOY equals Jesus and the word of God says the joy of the Lord is your strength. Hey, begin to laugh and have a little fun and realize that God loves you. Look for people around you that will love and care for you. When the residents I worked with began to have joy again, it would begin to bring motivation and freedom. In Jesus name, let joy be sparked in you and all you meet.

I was able to minister during devotion time in the nursing facilities to people who were beaten up inside because they thought they had to earn their salvation. Jesus paid for it all on the cross. I shared the scriptures that encouraged them to stop waiting till they were good enough because no one can ever be good enough. Giving Jesus your heart is the only way to be refreshed and rebuilt. The devil is the only one that wants to make you think that you have to earn your way to heaven. He will use past mistakes to convince you that you're not good enough. Jesus was the only one good enough and he lovingly paid the price for your sins. We can be a liberated people, freed by the blood of Jesus. He paid it all on the old rugged cross for you and me.

The word of God assures us that we're saved by grace through faith and never mentions that salvation comes by works. The word of God says, "Do not let your heart be troubled." (John 14:1a) You don't have to let your heart be troubled because you can trust in Jesus who has gone on ahead to prepare a place for us in heaven. I'm looking forward to it.

MASSAGE MINISTRY

As we begin a new phase of history in my life. The last five of the fifteen years in the nursing facility became very difficult although the vision and dreams of encouraging others would never stop. I sensed that a shift in my life was happening. I had been working part time at a hospital as well as in the nursing facilities and it began to be more than I could keep up with. I began talking to my boss in physical therapy and other therapists and they suggested that I go back to school for physical therapy or a massage therapist.

Although it was a tough decision, I went through school in 1999 and later began a new business. In January 2000 I prayerfully began "Jubilee Massage" which is still in operation. During the whole time I had to stay focused on what God wanted me to do. He was gracious enough to send encouragement through prophetic words, and people especially my very supportive wife. I thank God that I have a wonderful wife that stood behind me through everything. It was an incredible time of new challenges for a man of 50 going back to school and totally changing the direction of my life. God is good and He took care of all our needs and helped us to get through those times.

I believe it is important to share some of the prophetic words that were God's direction for the new stage in my life. In the summer of 1999, I was praying and seeking and even worrying about my decisions while making one of many commutes to school. Driving west on I-240 approaching Pennsylvania Ave, I received a clear word from the Lord which was confirmed by my wife Sandra and others. Number one was "you lay your hands on the sick and I will raise them up." Number two was "I will send you men and women of God to comfort and restore in mind, body, and spirit through therapeutic massage." Number three was "you are to rescue the perishing and care for the dying." I continue to hold these words in my heart, and through all of my life they still give me direction. God's word is still true and what he said he will do, he will do as I continue to stay in his will.

I just continued to press into God and He began to manifest healing mercies to many people. I give all the glory to God and am so humbled that he allowed me to be a vessel for him. So many times, people wanted me to pray for them and to this day there's not anybody that has ever come in for therapeutic massage that I haven't prayed for in the past 21 years. He told me to lay hands on the sick and he would heal them in heart, mind, body and soul, so that's what I did and continue to do.

Many times, people have opened their hearts, allowing Jesus to begin ministering to the wounds of their lives. They trusted in my confidentiality, and we trusted in God and stood on his divine and holy word. We saw many marriages restored, many healings, bound up people set free from past wounds and hurts and relief for those who are stressed and worn. The Holy Spirit just came down and did his work. It was never me. It was all Jesus. We just continue to reach out, encourage, pray for people and believe God to do a great and mighty work.

As I share these stories, I want you to keep in mind that our mission statement in our heart is the same as the Lord's is. Luke 4:18-19 says, "The Spirit of the Lord is on me, because he has anointed me to proclaim good news to the poor. He has sent me to proclaim freedom for the prisoners and recovery of sight for the blind, to set the oppressed free, to proclaim the year of the Lord's favor." The Spirit is upon us to bring the good news of the gospel to everyone.

One of the first massage stories I'll share is about a lady that came for a massage for the first time. Because of a history of abuse, she was full of fear. Her whole body was very tight, and she needed a lot of muscle work. Her husband came with her and sat there while she received her massage. She was not sure she could even tolerate a massage. I reassured her that I would do anything she wanted to help. She decided with her husband sitting back behind her and the massage room door opened that she would try. I began to pray for her through the massage and while loosening up the muscles and encouraging her that everything was gonna be alright. Jesus was right here with us and when he's in the room there's nothing he cannot do. Just like this woman, we have to get Jesus in the middle of our lives; in the middle of what we're doing and allow him to lead us and guide us. When we finished the massage, she was liberated and free and happy and comfortable and refreshed and restored. As we prayed and believed God with her and her husband, she was able to come out of her depression and all her fear. The Lord did a special work that day for that lady.

Another person who came for her first massage was a woman suffering from depression brought on through a series of bad situations. Before I began she said she had heard that I prayed for people. When I told her I did, she asked me to pray for her. She said she didn't want just one prayer but to pray the whole hour, so I began praying over her for the whole hour. That client has been coming for years now and every time she comes, she wants prayer for the whole hour! We both look forward to what God will do during that precious hour.

One of the things that I've noticed through the years is that you can't help somebody unless they want help. The mind is a very peculiar part of our body. In the word of God, it says we can have the mind of Christ when we surrender to him and give him first place in our life. When God comes down and we're born again, his spirit and our spirits are joined together making each one of us a new person. He begins to work and transform us by the word of God. Romans 12:2a states, "Do not conform to the pattern of this world, but be transformed by the renewing of your mind." A renewed mind will give a person new focus, new life and new direction. This new person can seek and find a new life by the Spirit. Zechariah 4:6b says, "'Not by might nor by power, but by my Spirit,' says the Lord Almighty."

One of my clients came to try a massage for the pain in her diseased body. She was very nervous, so her daughter brought her in to help her. Because of her modesty, I worked only where she was comfortable. We began to pray and believe God for healing mercies and as I worked on her she started opening up to me. We began to share life's experiences, especially what the Lord had done through the years for each of us. As we agreed in prayer that day God kept his promise of where two agree as touching anything, he will do it. Each time she came, we believed God in prayer and bound our hearts together to stand on the authority of the word of God. That day and many days afterwards she received refreshment, motivation, strength and real pain relief. She came for years all through the rest of her days, and I was able to minister to my dear friend and her family.

There are so many stories like my friend where people were all locked up and unmotivated. It is my humble privilege to have been able to encourage these people, pray for them, and let them know that someone really cared about them. The therapeutic massage is a way to open the door to build a trusting relationship. We believed God to get them through whatever obstacles were in the way.   Praise God the opportunities were there, and I was able to stand by them and believe God to get them through.

I had a client, pregnant in her eighth month, and the baby was hibernating in the area of her hip causing great discomfort. The woman's mother brought her in, and I started praying for her. I didn't know what I was supposed to do, but the Lord did, and he led me to a particular technique. I began to pray for her also and within five minutes she was fine! Everything was great, and we believe in God to do it again because he's always on time and never late.

Many times, through the years God just continued to do what he did as we believed in and stood on the word of God. To believe and not be afraid to lay hands on the sick to see them recover is at the heart of my mission. God begins and the impossible happens. Miracles become a reality. If we all stand on the word of God found in 2 Timothy 1:7 (NKJ), "For God has not given us a spirit of fear, but of power and of love and of a sound mind." The sound mind in that scripture means self control. It is not us but the Holy Spirit that gives the sound mind and allows us also to have the mind of Christ. Philippians 2:5 (NKJV) admonishes, "Let this mind be in you which was also in Christ Jesus" to go forth with a self-disciplined, sound mind and be overcomers.

We overcomers are covered by the blood of the lamb and by the word of our testimony. As we begin to line our word up with the word of God, it changes what we speak out of our mouth. Out of the abundance of your heart your mouth speaks; so not speaking doubt and fear, or having worry, anxiety, gloom, and doom we can build ourselves up with the word of God. That is the overcoming part of life. It is not at all easy but as we press into prayer, follow God's word and sing his praises; there's not anything that the lying devil can do about it. We are victorious no matter if we pass from this life; we are promised new life and a brand new glorious body like Jesus. "For our citizenship is in heaven, from which we also eagerly wait for the Savior, the Lord Jesus Christ, who will transform our lowly body that it may be conformed to His glorious body, according to the working by which He is able even to subdue all things to Himself." Philippians 3:20,21 (NKJ)

MIRACLES

As we begin this last section is going to be on miracles that I have seen with my eyes. I realize that God does miracles every day in different ways. Creation is a miracle. A newborn baby is a miracle. These are just two examples of what many would say are miracles, but I want to talk to you about a different miracle. I'm talking about an instant manifestation of God, where God takes something wrong and makes it right by the blood of Jesus to see with your eyes the manifestation of God transforming a person to fresh life and healing by the blood of Jesus will transform your faith. My hope and prayer is that you have an opportunity to experience that kind of miracle.

I would like to refer back to the young lady in the nursing home who doctors said would never walk or speak again. God had different plans for her and as I prayed and spoke God's word over her, he began to move. I knew in my gut when I was working with her that God was going to do something great. I never gave up and never stopped believing and praying for her. Her family moved her before I got to see the completed work. God was gracious enough to send her to my door about a year or two later after I had begun the massage business in ministry. On that memorable summer afternoon, she told me who she was and wanted to thank me for never giving up and continually praying for her. She said she could hear me but couldn't respond and She began verifying all the scriptures and prayers she heard. She knew I was working with her and all the details of that. It was quite an experience to hear her share how thankful and grateful she was that she was completely whole. You could have blown me over with a feather that afternoon, as I was very grateful to see the manifestation of what God can do.

I also got to experience God's miracle working power in my own mother's life. I was told when I was 9 that she wouldn't live much longer because of the disease she fought all her life. I want to share a miracle with you that happened right before my very eyes when I was 14. It was a summer afternoon, I was sitting there with my mother who 5 years later was still defying the medical world by continuing to live, and she asked me a question. "I don't want you to think I'm crazy, but I want you to do something for me that's going to be different." I said, "Well whatever you need, I'll try mother. I love you and it's OK."

She said "As I was reading scriptures and studying the word of God that I heard The Lord speak to me and I know God wants me to get on the floor because He is going to do some healing. I don't understand it but I want to obey what he wants me to do" and I said "well mother if you feel like that's what you need to do I'll be glad to help you." So, as we got on the floor I helped her down there. We were sitting there together and stayed down there for about 30 minutes. She said, "Well it's done, and I can get back in the bed now." I helped her back to bed. She had epilepsy so she had seizures daily and medicine for that, but when she got back in the bed that day God had healed her completely. No more seizures and no more seizure medicine and she never had another seizure. She never did have to take any more of the seizure medicine and you don't get off that medicine instantly either. When my dad got home everything was fine, and he was glad. They had a good fellowship. She told her doctor what she had done and that it was all right because she was all right. So, I saw with my eyes the manifestation of a miracle by God's love for her. She knew Jesus Christ as her personal Savior and Lord and God came down that afternoon and gave her a miracle from all seizures and medication.

There are many miracles and types such as progressive type miracles-progressive healings. Many things can describe the healing mercies of Jesus. The word of God asks in Isaiah "Who will believe the report of the Lord?" Isaiah 53:1-6, it explains that by his stripes you were and are healed. What he did on Calvary paid the price for our salvation, for our healing and for the goodness of God dwelling in us and transforming us every day. So, there's many types of miracles, but it's such a blessing to see with your eyes the manifestation of the healing mercies of a living God that dwells in us today.

PRINCIPLES TO LIVE BY

We know we have an exciting God that is always there every day. He's a great almighty God who gave us his son on the cross, that through his death, burial and resurrection we have a living hope within us. He is providing living hope and he loves you and wants you to be set free. He wants you in his word reading and building yourself up in his word every day. I encourage you this day to accept Jesus Christ as your Lord and Savior and let him be THE REFUGE that you run to. He's got a lot of good things for you. We have a wonderful and great and mighty God, and I challenge each one of you today to begin to feed yourself on the word of God, meditate on the word of God day and night as it says in Psalms 1:2b. Psalms 46:10a says "to be still and know that I am God." Go ahead and spend time with Jesus and be in that quiet time with him.

Ephesians 1:3 tells us we are blessed with every spiritual blessing in heavenly places. The Lord showed me a couple of years ago that we're actually seated with him in high places. You can just wrap yourself up in him and climb up in his lap and just be with him. He'll just stroke your head and hold you and love you. He loves you so much! Just let it all go and let him have it because he knows so much more than we do. He can do anything, even a life changing miracle in your life. He can continue to do miracles in my life. He wants to set us free and liberate us to be the people of God and do his work and his will on this earth today. God loves you very much and he told us in the great commission found in Matthew:28. "All authority in heaven and on earth has been given to me. 19 Therefore go and make disciples of all nations, baptizing them in the name of the Father and of the Son and of the Holy Spirit, 20 and teaching them to obey everything I have commanded you. And surely I am with you always, to the very end of the age.`` You need to focus on Jesus Christ and him crucified. He is your savior, lord, master, redeemer, and the king of glory, Hebrews chapter 13:8 says Jesus Christ is the same yesterday today and forever and to seek him with all your heart because of what he has done for you. We are sons of God through faith in Christ. There is neither Jew nor Greek, slave or free, male or a female; you are all one in Christ Jesus. Galatians 3:26-28. Jesus loves everyone- red, yellow, black, and white are all precious in his sight. Our God that we serve is colorblind. Our Jesus has washed us clean by his blood and forgives everyone.

I want to encourage you today to receive food for your spirit, soul and body. The body is the outermost man while the soul is the mind, will and emotions. Our spirit is the inner man. We're all a three part being so I want to encourage you today to make sure you have accepted Jesus Christ as your Savior and Lord.

As we look into the word of God, I want you to look at different versions of the Bible and you'll find that will help you to better understand. For example, John 3:16 tells us "For God so loved the world that he gave his only begotten son, that whosoever believes in him shall be saved." As we read the word of God in different versions it helps you to understand and see things clearly as the Holy Spirit will lead you and guide you into all truth.

So, as I share with you, I want to encourage you to make sure that you know Jesus Christ as your personal savior. The Amplified Version, John 3:3 states, . . . "I assure you and most solemnly say to you, unless a person is born again [reborn from above—spiritually transformed, renewed, sanctified], he cannot [ever] see and experience the kingdom of God." So we must be born again to experience the things of God. Romans 3:23 says "for all have sinned and come short of the glory of God." No person is without sin so it is not wrong for you to go ahead and admit that we are so that we can be forgiven by the blood of Jesus. Because Jesus suffered on the cross -bled and died and rose again- we can receive his mercy and grace. The Amplified Version of 1John 1:9 states "to freely admit we have sinned and confess our sins and he is faithful and just, true to his own nature and promises, and will forgive our sins dismiss our lawlessness and continuously cleanse us from all unrighteousness everything not in conformity to his will in purpose thought and action."

Step one is receiving Christ by admitting that we are sinners, that we invite him to come into our hearts and confess him as Savior and Lord. This means to speak to him for he hears and answers our prayers as we submit our hearts to him and ask him to forgive us and cleanse us. As we receive Jesus Christ as our personal Lord and Savior we have salvation. Romans 10:9 tells us that if we confess with our mouth Jesus is Lord and believe with our hearts that God raised him from the dead we will be saved. At that point we have decided to believe in the word of God that Jesus Christ came to live, bleed and die for our sins.

When we invite him in our hearts according to scripture and say to him that we believe he is the son of God who died was raised from the dead and that we want Jesus to come in our hearts and live there. Romans 10:10 says with the heart a person believes and is justified. Justified means just as if you never sinned. The word of God makes it clear to us that we are washed by Jesus's blood shed on the cross for you and for me. This is the gospel that the word of God talks about in I Corinthians 15:2-3, "By this gospel you are saved, if you hold firmly to the word I preached to you. Otherwise, you have believed in vain. For what I received I passed on to you as of first importance: that Christ died for our sins according to the Scriptures."

As we progress, I'd like to give you some scriptures to read and study. We talked about being born again in John 3:3. Genesis 1:1 shows us that in the beginning God spoke everything into existence. Hebrews 11:6 says without faith it is impossible to please God. And Hebrews 11: 1 tells you what faith is.

Matthew 1:18-23 tells us that Jesus is the son of God, born of a virgin in the flesh and blood. Jesus is God - one part of the Trinity - one part of the triune Godhead. Colossians 2:9 and Hebrews 1:5-8 support the fact that he came in a fleshly body so he could help man. John 1:14, Luke 4:18-21 show how he took on himself all your sins and bore them on his own body when he died on the cross.

Isaiah 53:4-5, 2Corinthians 5:21 show that he died for your sins. Luke 24:1-7 tells how God raised him from the dead. Acts 2:32 and Hebrews 10:12 tells us that he is now seated at the right hand of the father in heaven. Why do I want you to read the word of God? The word of God says that faith comes by hearing and hearing by the word of God. The word of God said faith is the knowledge of things hoped for and the evidence of things not seen. This is found in Hebrews 11:1 and Hebrews 11:6 says it is impossible to please God without faith. Therefore, we must commit ourselves to the authority of the word of God and receive what the Holy Spirit is teaching us. He loves us and cares for us and wants to show us strength as we trust him, live for him and follow him all the days of our lives.

Make sure that you have followed through with being born again. How are we born again? We invite Jesus to come into our heart. James 4 says that you have not because you asked not. As we talked about and shared already, get somewhere quiet and listen to what God is saying to you. He loves you so much and cares for you no matter what is going on to the left or the right in our lives. Psalms 46 says be still and know that I am God. Listen to his voice and he will feed you on the word of God. He will begin to love you and minister to your heart and mind as he draws you to himself.

I want to walk alongside you right now. Just reaffirm that you have prayed and invited Jesus into your heart and ask him to forgive your sins. He will forgive you and he will come to live in your spirit and your spirit will come alive in God. I encourage you right now to pour out your heart to God in your own way and pray to him. For example, you may say something as simple as "Father God, I believe Jesus is your son - the Savior of the world. I believe he died on the cross for my sins. I need you Jesus. I receive you by faith. Forgive my sins and save me. Please come to live inside me. I want to be born again."

If you cry out to him, you will receive all that he has for you. You are now a new creature in Christ. 2 Corinthians 5:17 conveys that now you are in a right relationship with God, and in 5:21 see how we can become righteous because of Christ. Read those things and receive from him what he said even if you don't feel anything. Don't worry about feeling just know that as you've been obedient to the word of God in your life and have lived your life before him, you can receive what God says.

Jesus said in John 14:6, "I am the way and the truth and the life. No one comes to the Father except through me." Acts 4:12 about tells us that salvation is found under no other name than Jesus. Don't listen to anything other than the authority found in the word of God. Be encouraged today that you have a living God. He's alive and well and his son Jesus Christ is in you now.

Begin to feed yourself on the word of God and grow in Christ. You have an experience now in the new birth as a Christian following Jesus with all of your heart and mind, so begin to feed yourself on the word of God. Ask him to feed you on his word so your spirit and soul can receive strength from him. Begin to walk in his divine and holy word in order to grow in Christ.

It's so important to follow him, read his word every day and feed yourself on the word of God. We get to walk with him, talk with him and live with him. You have a new friend, and he'll never leave you nor forsake you. John 14:16 talks about how he is there for you and will always be by your side.

As you begin to walk with him another step in that walk is water baptism. The word of God teaches that to be baptized, According to Romans 6:4, we need to be dipped, plunged or immersed - to be buried in water and raised to walk in the newness of life. The same resurrection power that raised Jesus from the dead is what you get. This is also confirmed in 1 Peter 3:21. Read Acts 2:37-38 to see how on the day of Pentecost they heard the word of God and repented which means to do a turnabout, change, and go another direction. Repentance means to make an about face in life and go to a new direction. Be baptized in water and receive the Holy Spirit so you can begin to walk with him and draw yourself under him every day in Christ.

As you begin your walk with God, it's important that you receive sound spiritual teachings regarding the basics of the word of God. Feed yourself on the word always and live in God's word, for it teaches us in his word that we are to walk as a follower of the truth, allowing him to feed us on his divine and holy word. Remember that the word of God teaches Jesus Christ and him crucified. Look to the authority of the word of God that tells us who Christ is and what he's done for us. Anything that teaches differently is not from God.

Jesus Christ and him crucified is the authority of the message. Remember Jesus said "I am the way, the truth and the life and no man comes to the father except by me." We must learn to receive the authority of the word of God to progress in our walk with him and begin to receive all that he has for us in the authority of his word.

Also, as you progress in the word of God and feed yourself on the word of God you can prepare to receive the baptism of the Holy Spirit. This is also a part of our walk with God. Acts 1:8 tells us that when the Holy Spirit comes upon us, we are to be witnesses throughout the world. The baptism of the Holy Spirit allows you and me to have the power in Christ and to go and administer the love of Jesus to others.

Now it's very important for us to know what love is and to give God's love to people all around us. We must give God's love out of our hearts to others. Doctrine doesn't mean anything without God's love. John 3:16-17 are very well-known verses about the love of God toward the world. God sent not his son into the world to condemn, but to save. Everybody can be saved through him. It's not about a doctrine - it's about giving God's precious love to everyone around us.

Everything we do should be according to the foundation of the authority of the gospel. Read 1 Corinthians 15: 1-4 to see what the gospel is. Jesus said in Matthew 28:18-19 "All authority in heaven and on earth has been given to me. Therefore, go and make disciples of all nations, baptizing them in the name of the Father and of the Son and of the Holy Spirit." That is the direction of the heartbeat of God - nothing else. The power of the baptism of the Holy Spirit is ministering the love of Jesus and sharing God's heart of love with the world around us. It's not for any other reason. God's heart is full of love for all those he created but to understand it better see what he says in the word. Study 1 Corinthians 13. We must love people where they're at for them to receive the things of God. We must have a pure heart of love and care and respect for people. From this pure heart and with the right attitude, we can minister the love of Jesus.

As we begin studying God's word, I want to encourage you to make sure you have a Bible where you can read every day. Get a variety of different versions of the Bible. The English Standard Version is an excellent Bible that features references from The Strong's Exhaustive Concordance and even a Bible dictionary making it a good foundational Bible. The Amplified Bible gives greater explanation in each verse about what the word of God is saying. Other versions that are helpful are the New King James and The Revised Standard Version. There are many versions but having one with study helps is important. A paraphrase is going to give you a phrase to explain a subject but is generally the interpretation of one or two people; so in due respect it is not translating word to word from the Greek, Hebrew or Aramaic. These paraphrased Bibles are ok- just be careful. It will give you a thought over a subject but it's not a translation.

The important thing is to study the word of God and pray the word of God. Ask the Holy Spirit to lead you and guide you into all truth with accuracy. You will know the truth and the truth will set you free. As we begin to study about the love of God and to know him as your personal savior, we can be assured that he lives in us and cares for us so much that he'll make a way for us. Our responsibility is to continually feed ourselves all the word of God; so that we know him and can serve him. That's what it is all about.

We're going to go into some study things as we begin to read and give some foundations for studying the word of God in order to know him better. In 1John 1:1-5 you get to know that you know that you know that Jesus Christ is your savior and lord and now that you're going to heaven because the blood of Jesus has provided you a place with him. John chapter 14 says to not let your heart be troubled for he has provided you a heavenly home. John 14:6 God wants you to know that Jesus is the way, the truth and the life and no man comes to the Father except by him.

As you begin to study and know Jesus intimately as your Savior and Lord, the word of God becomes closer to you, next to your heart, and bonds to you as you serve him and love him with everything within you. It will be a one day at a time experience. Luke 9:23 that to walk with Jesus, we must lay down our life daily. It's a daily experience - not a Sunday to Sunday or special holidays to go to church. It's a daily 365 days a year, 24 hours a day, seven days a week commitment to experiencing the living God. Acts 4:12 talks about how salvation is found in no other name but Jesus Christ the one that died on the cross and rose from the grave. In 1 Corinthians 15:1-3 we see that the gospel is all about the death, burial and resurrection of Jesus. Bond yourself with the truth and be set free.

We're going into an area here just to give you some foundational things as a born-again believer. When you have accepted Jesus Christ as your personal savior these foundations and the power of God will begin to grow in you. As you grow in God and take a daily walk with him, you're going to experience Jesus. You're gonna know him as your savior, lord, master and redeemer.

Psalms 1 talks about meditating on the word of God day and night. It's not a weekly thing but a constant feast on all the word of God. Romans 12 talks about not being conformed to the things of this world but being transformed by the renewing of our minds with the word of God. Philippians 3 talks about having the mind of Christ. The only way we can have the mind of Christ is to feed ourselves all his word. Then it will be his mind and his heart that fills us with his love, his mercy and his grace. This is accomplished when reading and studying the word of God not once a week and not just when we say we have time, but we must discipline ourselves as a child of God to meditate daily on his divine, holy word.

In this next section I would like to share some foundational Bible principles. I will be sharing quite a bit, and sometimes adding just what's on my heart. As I share my heart with you through all the stories and all the foundation of my life. As a 73-year-old man I have made many mistakes, but thank God for 1John 1:9 that says when we ask forgiveness, he forgives us and doesn't want us to dwell on it but to move on. When you make a mistake or do something you should not, don't wait till you see the preacher, get to church or pray your nightly prayers, but get forgiveness right away - right where you are. You will make a mistake. We're all going to make mistakes because we live in this physical body. We're not going to be perfect till we get to heaven when we will get a brand new glorious body. Philippians 3:20-21 tells us that, so we know that if we make a mistake, we get forgiveness. Don't ever let anybody tell you that you have to get somebody else to ask God to forgive you of your sins because now that's not scripture. Through Christ we can go directly to God. We must line up what we know and what we believe with the word of God. You don't need to receive any confusion. We have to be kind and not rude to people, but we can speak the truth in love. In John chapter 8:32 God says you'll know the truth and be set free.

We must begin to line ourselves up with the word of God and love other people so they can love Jesus too. The only way they're going to love Jesus and know him as a personal savior is for you to be the church until they will go to church. Many times, people don't want to go to church just to listen to someone preach. They have no reason to until they have a heart for change. That's why they have to see Jesus Christ in us before they are going to want to go. Sometimes we can get somebody to go but the intent of the heart of God is for us to share the love of Jesus with everybody around us. People have to see Jesus in us before they're going to want to go to church or do anything about their spiritual condition.

To be able to share Jesus effectively, it is good to have a solid foundation. I would like to share some foundational principles and ways to share Jesus with others. It is good to start at the beginning as it states in Genesis 1:1 "In the beginning God created the heavens and the earth." As referenced in Hebrews 11:3, it's by faith we understand that God is the one who spoke the universe into existence. Secondly, Jesus is the son of God who was born of a virgin, born and became flesh and blood and dwelt among us. Matthew 1:23 repeats the words of the prophet Isiah who foretold that Jesus would be born of a virgin. Thirdly, Jesus is God, one part of the Trinity made up of God the father, Jesus the son, and the Holy Spirit. Colossians 2:9 states "For in Christ all the fullness of the Deity lives in bodily form." Be sure to read Hebrews 1:5-8 that further establishes how God views Jesus his son.

Fourthly Jesus came in a fleshly body so he could help man. John 1:1,14 and Luke 4:18-21 show us Jesus on this earth as flesh and blood. Isaiah 53:4-5, 2 Corinthians 5:11 and Hebrews 2:9 reveal to us how Jesus chose to follow God's will and take on himself all our sins, to bear them on his own body to the cross, where he willingly died for all our sins. Luke 24:1-7 shows us the next step when God raised Jesus from the dead. Acts 2:32 confirms this as well.

After being raised from the dead, according to Hebrews 10:12 Jesus is seated at the right hand of the Father in heaven where he is available to every person who will believe. He will come to live in your human spirit by the power and the presence of the Holy Spirit making you a child of God as stated in Romans 8:14-16. This is what it means to accept Jesus Christ as your savior, and if you believe these things then you truly understand that you were a sinner in need of a savior. Romans 3:23-24 tells us that all have come short of God's glory, and if we confess our sins, he assures us in 1 John 1:9 that he will forgive us.

Having an attitude of repentance and willingly turning from your sin allows you to live a new life for God. Acts 3:19 tells us the new life will be followed with times of refreshing. Then we can begin praying. James 4:2 says you have not because you ask not. Ask Jesus to forgive your sins and he will forgive you. He will come to live in your spirit and your spirit will come alive.

I encourage you to pour out your heart to God in your own way around this formula. You can say "Father God, I believe Jesus Christ is your son, the savior of the world. I believe he died on the cross for me and bore all my sins. I believe Jesus was resurrected from the dead and is now at the right hand of God. I need you Jesus. I receive you by faith; forgive my sins and Lord come live inside of me. I want to be born again." If you have prayed that prayer, then congratulations to you! You have accepted Jesus Christ as your savior and are a new creature. According to 2 Corinthians 5:17, 21 you're now in the right relationship with God and in Jesus have become the righteousness of God.

People have different reactions to this life changing experience of new birth. Whether you have an emotional reaction or not is dependent on each individual experience. If you have willingly accepted Jesus Christ as your savior, you may or may not experience big vibes. Some people express the feeling of cleansing or relief since their burden has been lifted. I encourage you to remember that the Bible does not tell us to have our faith on feelings, but you must know in your heart you accepted him as your savior. I want to encourage you personally as you begin to walk with him and serve him. I promise you; you're going to feel some things once in a while. When his presence is all around you, you're going to know that you know that you know he is real. Just accept his presence as a reward for your faith in him. There will be times when you just have a special moment of time with him and feel him and grow in him. You just feel his love and his mercy and grace. I encourage you to be filled and strengthened with the mercy and the goodness of God. He is so good! As we align our words up with him and his words, we can begin to walk in the authority of his love and mercy and grace.

Now as you feed yourself on the Word of God and embrace the principles of being born again found in John chapter 3:3-5; of cleansing by the washing of water through the word in Ephesians 5:26; and the word of God that lives in, abides in us forever found in 1 Peter 1:23. We will begin to line our word up with his word. Romans 10:8-10 tells us that the word is near you, within your mouth and heart. Jesus said out of the abundance of your heart, your mouth speaks. You will begin to walk in his authority, and in the abundance of his grace through faith.

As you study that born-again experience, you can begin to share with others 2 Corinthians 5:17 which shows how they can become a new creation if they cry out to God, and he will make all the past fall away so all things will become new. At this point we're joyfully entering the kingdom of God as we walk with him according to Colossians 1:12-13.

Another foundational principle is that we are a three part being containing the body, the soul, and the spirit. We know that our body contains the five senses of feel, touch, taste, sight, and smell. We know that our soul contains the mind, will, and emotions. We know the third part, the spirit, sometimes known as the inner man, is where we can join together with God's spirit.

One of the biggest challenges for any believer is control. Although it doesn't feel like it sometimes, we are daily in control of our bodies. To govern the body, we must have the mind of Christ because it is impossible to do it without him. If we have the mind of Christ, then we can align our will to God's will and bring our emotions in order. His emotions become our emotions. In the spirit man, our inner man, we are born again. God comes down by his spirit to join together with us so that we know who we are in Christ.

As you read, study and review with me about being born again and how you are the righteousness of God in Christ, study these things out in your study Bibles. Other points of study are how our faith makes us whole, healing is for you now as is the baptism of the Holy Spirit. The Holy Spirit was given for the power of the gospel to be shared throughout the world. Study how we have victorious, abundant life in Christ as we serve him, confess his word, and align our words up with his words. This brings the authority of the word of God as we live for him.

Learn through the word about the picture created by water baptism. Water baptism is an outward sign of an inward change. You have received Christ as your personal Savior and Lord and now you want to obey him by being immersed in a watery grave and being raised out of it into new life. Jesus gives us instruction about baptism in Matthew 28:19, Mark 16:15-16, Acts 2:38. Saul became Paul and was baptized after his conversion in Acts 9:18. In Acts 19:1-6 Cornelius' household was baptized after which they received the Holy Spirit. In Acts 10:44-48 Peter preached and the people were filled with the Spirit and baptized with water.

Studying your Bible helps you to know who you are or where you're going in Christ. We know that 1 John 5:13 says that you may know that you have eternal life and that you are the righteousness of God in Christ. Romans 5:17-21 tells about how one man, Adam, sinned and brought death to reign on the earth while another man, Jesus, did not sin and brought grace to reign through righteousness bringing eternal life for any who choose to receive it. Review again Romans 5:17 For if, by the trespass of the one man, death reigned through that one man, how much more will those who receive God's abundant provision of grace and of the gift of righteousness reign in life through the one man, Jesus Christ .

Jesus bore our sins and we know that according to scripture shows us that will build yourself on the word of God the reality of the truth that set you free 2 Corinthians 5:21 we had made him who do you know saying to be sin for us that we might become the righteousness of God in him. Righteousness means a right relationship with the living God. That's what that means so you can begin the walk in the authority and the blood of Jesus as you serve him.

Romans 3:21-24 states, "But now apart from the law the righteousness of God has been made known, to which the Law and the Prophets testify. 22 This righteousness is given through faith in[h] Jesus Christ to all who believe. There is no difference between Jew and Gentile, 23 for all have sinned and fall short of the glory of God, 24 and all are justified freely by his grace through the redemption that came by Christ Jesus." Romans 10:10-11 tells us that when we believe in our hearts and confess with our mouth he will take away our shame. Remember it is so important for us to stop the devil from bringing up the past because we have been justified and become not guilty because of the blood of Jesus that was shed for us according to Romans 5:9. In Romans 8:1-4 emphatically states that there is no condemnation to those who are in Christ Jesus who do not walk according to the flesh but according to the spirit.

In Christ I know there's no fear. You need to memorize 2 Timothy 1:7 - "For the Spirit God gave us does not make us timid, but gives us power, love and self-discipline." This verse is critically important to your walk in God. God has not given us a spirit of fear but of power, love and a sound mind. Begin to walk in the victory and authority of Christ. The Holy Spirit guides us in self-discipline to a sound mind by the power of God in Christ.

Galatians 2:20 is another very important verse to memorize. "I have been crucified with Christ and I no longer live, but Christ lives in me. The life I now live in the body, I live by faith in the Son of God, who loved me and gave himself for me." Remember that the blood of Jesus Christ God's son cleanses us from all sin and Jesus is coming again.

The scriptures are so important to memorize so we can battle against the havoc the devil tries to force into your mind. He'll remind you of past mistakes to convince you that you are no good and will never be good enough to be let into heaven. The devil is a liar! John 10:10 tells us how the devil comes to kill, steal and destroy but Jesus comes to give abundant l

As you study the word you will see that Jesus experienced temptation in the wilderness as he was tempted by the devil in Matthew 4 :1-11 One main issue that I would like to bring out is in verse 4 which says We are to live by every word that comes from the mouth of God which is God's word the Bible. Also, another scripture in line with that is 2 Timothy 3 :16 which starts out saying all scriptures are inspired. The Greek word means God breathed on every word.

Begin to speak the word of God over yourself and build your faith. Your faith has made you whole. To fight the good fight of faith and become a faith warrior, it is necessary to study scriptures on faith. Start with Hebrews 11:1 that explains how faith is the knowledge of things hoped for, the evidence of things not seen. There are three power principles in faith -- the knowledge of his word, acting upon his word, and trusting he'll bring the word of God alive in you.

Hebrews 11:6 tells us that without faith it is impossible to please God, and Romans 10:17 emphasizes that faith comes by hearing and hearing by the word of God. We have to keep our faith, our dependency in Jesus Christ and him crucified in order to walk in the authority of His love. Act on his word every day. This acting on his word will bring you to a deeper understanding of Jesus Christ as our Savior, Lord, Master, and Redeemer.

We must focus our spiritual eyes on God's word. It is his inspired word which means that God breathed on it, and it became alive. Memorize 2 Timothy 3:16-17, "All Scripture is God-breathed and is useful for teaching, rebuking, correcting and training in righteousness, so that the servant of God may be thoroughly equipped for every good work." Try to do that because that is the authority of God that we are healed as is referenced in Psalm 103:2-3. We can proclaim this word of God's healing over ourselves and be healed. Speak this word of faith over yourself. When you bless the Lord, you reap the benefits of his forgiveness and his healing.

Believe the report of the Lord found in Isaiah 53. An intense study of this chapter will show you more fully who Jesus is, was, and will be for all mankind. Those who believe this report of the Lord walk in victory not defeat. This rich chapter tells us how Jesus bore our sins on the cross and by every horrible stripe that was laid on his back, we are healed.

This message of healing is reiterated in Matthew 8:16-17 also shows us how Jesus spoke the word and healed the sick, even drove out demons. Jesus showed us as believers we can speak God's word in faith and see miracles happen. Daily feeding on his word and immersing ourselves in it will bring us to a deeper understanding of this authority to speak God's word and see wonderful things happen. When we dedicate all our hearts and all our minds and all of our souls to the word of God, his truth will bring us to greater understanding.

This greater understanding opens our eyes to see the true author of sickness and disease. We know that Satan is the author of the evil in this world. His presence on earth happened when Adam sinned in the Garden of Eden. Before Adam sinned in the garden there was no Satan on the earth but after his disobedience, death with all its evil companions of hatred, bitterness, jealousy, sickness, disease, and torment came to all people. Roman 5:12 shows us that Jesus was to reestablish the wholeness that man had before the fall. He was the redeemer; the one sent to buy you back from the dominion of Satan. Acts 10:38 shows us how God anointed Jesus with the Holy Spirit and power to do good by healing and freeing oppressed people from the devil. God wants us to prosper and be in good health. This is shown in 3 John 2. In 1 Corinthians 6:20 we are told that we were bought with a price and to glorify God with our bodies.

We see that we are redeemed from the curse and promised the spirit in Galatians 3:13-14. Memorize this very important verse of faith found in Hebrews 13:8, "Jesus Christ is the same yesterday, today, and forever." A very, very important prayer of faith anointing can be found in Mark 11:22 -24. John 16:23-24, Matthew 18:18-20, Mark 16:18, James 5:14-15, Exodus 15:26, Psalms 103:3, 1Peter 2:24, Matthew 8:16-17 are more important verses to study and they can guide you in a walk of faith. I especially like James 5:14-15 that states, "Is anyone among you sick? Let them call the elders of the church to pray over them and anoint them with oil in the name of the Lord. And the prayer offered in faith will make the sick person well; the Lord will raise them up. If they have sinned, they will be forgiven." We asked Jesus to forgive us of our sins and he is faithful and just to do that as we have already seen in 1John 1:9.

Another aspect of walking with God involves the Holy Spirit. There are many scriptures you can study in the word of God about the Holy Spirit like Matthew 3:11, Acts 1:4-5, John 3:16, and Galatians 5:17. Titus 3:5 (KJV) that it is "Not by works of righteousness which we have done, but according to his mercy he saved us, by the washing of regeneration, and renewing of the Holy Ghost." As we read and receive the word of God by the Holy Spirit, we can say that Jesus is Lord only by the Holy Spirit according to 1Corinthians 12:3. Romans 8:16 tells us that The Spirit himself bears witness with our spirits that we are children of God. Genesis 1:2 says that the Spirit hovered over the waters at the creation of the earth. Joel 2:28-29 tells us how God will pour out his Spirit on everyone and powerful dreams and visions will be produced. John 7:37-39 gives us Jesus's promise that if we are thirsty, we can believe and receive rivers of living water (the Holy Spirit). The Holy Spirit is a comforter and teacher of the truth in John 14:16-17 and 15:26. We know that He is our helper.

When we begin to speak his truth over ourselves and the people around us and begin to serve him and love him and be filled with the Holy Spirit. John 15:7 says to ask and you will receive. Scriptures teach about speaking in tongues and this is why it's so critical for us as believers to line our words up by the word of God. In Acts 2 the 120 believers spoke with all the languages of the day but as they received the baptism of the Holy Spirit, they understood all that was spoken and spoke in another tongue. The Gentiles in the house of Cornelius spoke with other tongues when the Holy Spirit came on them in Acts 10:44-46. In Acts 9:17, Paul was filled with the Holy Spirit after Ananias laid hands on him. He later told an assembly of Christians that he spoke in tongues more than they did. 1 Corinthians 14:4 he said anyone praying in the spirit edifies and builds himself up. He goes on to conclude in 14:39-40, " Therefore, brethren, desire earnestly to prophesy, and do not forbid to speak with tongues. Let all things be done decently and in order."

What is a manifestation of the spirit? In 1Corinthians 12 we see a chapter filled with foundational principles regarding the gifts of the spirit given to each one in the body of believers. Look now at the gifts listed in verses 7-10. The various gifts of the Spirit build up the body of Christ. Each person may at different times minister with a number of gifts in the Spirit that are found in Roman 12:5-8, but we know of course every believer does not operate in all the gifts all the time. The gifts of the Spirit are manifest to meet needs as they arise. Several gifts may come forth at one time in a body of believers, but it is the Spirit who administers as he wills. At the same time, the believer must allow himself to be used and directed by the Spirit. The Spirit is always going to be in order, for God does not create confusion but gives peace as is referenced in 1 Corinthians 14:32-33. An order is given to us in 1 Corinthians 12:28-30 regarding public ministry of these spiritual gifts to avoid confusion. 1 Corinthians14 verse 4-5 tells us, "He who speaks in a tongue edifies himself, but he who prophesies edifies the church. I wish you all spoke with tongues, but even more that you prophesied; for he who prophesies is greater than he who speaks with tongues, unless indeed he interprets, that the church may receive edification." All things done decently and in order is supremely important so look at the simple truth stated in 1 Corinthians 14:40. So that gives you some study guides on tongues if you're looking for the truth to set you free from any confusion or misunderstanding.

Another direction for your victorious, abundant life that we have in Christ starts by looking at 1 John 5:4-5 which tells us that those born of God overcome the world and this is the victory. We have overcome the world through our faith that Jesus is the son of God. You become an overcomer because the one in you, Jesus, overcame the world as stated in 1John 4:4. The devil wants to distract you; Jesus wants to motivate you. As we seek to live for Jesus and serve him, I encourage you to put on the full armor of God found in Ephesians 6:13-18. It is critically important for you to stay there and understand what the armor is and how to put it on daily. In 2 Corinthians 10:4-5, the believer's weapons of warfare are not flesh but divine, demolishing strongholds or anything that exalts itself against the knowledge of God and bringing every thought into captivity. John 10:10 tells the thief comes to devastate and annihilate, but Jesus comes to bring life more abundantly. The abundant life in Christ is still true for you today.

In Romans 8:16-17 we find that as a believer we have a joint inheritance with Christ as testified by the Spirit. It further states that if we suffer with him, we are also glorified together with him. God has freely given all things, even his own son so that we might live as sons and daughters with all the rights that are related to an heir.

The next part of this study guide has to do with spiritual blessing. Look at Ephesians 1:3, "Praise be to the God and Father of our Lord Jesus Christ, who has blessed us in the heavenly realms with every spiritual blessing in Christ." The Lord gave me an encouraging vision a couple of years ago, when you're praying and seeking God, and you read that verse you are seated with him in a special place. I believe it reflects the intimacy we have in Jesus in that place. You can pray and you can crawl up into your Father God's lap. You can envision yourself sharing a quiet time with him. Psalms 46 tells us "Be still and know that I am God." Crawl up in his lap and begin to let him hold you. Picture him stroking your hair and just let yourself rest in his mercy and his grace. Believe his hands are on you and just rest in him and his goodness. You can just be built up in him and seated with him. Memorize that verse as you go to him in prayer every day. Psalms 23 establishes the Lord as shepherd, a protective wall, and everything we need. Be encouraged today, believe it. I pray that you prosper in all things as your soul prospers.

Another aspect of blessing is in Philippians 4:19 where "God shall supply all your needs according to his riches in glory." He wants to bless you today as you feed yourself on the word of God. 2 Corinthians 9:8 assures us that "God is able to bless you abundantly, so that in all things at all times, having all that you need, you will abound in every good work." He wants you to do well when serving him with all your heart and mind. Confessing the word of God over yourself daily is very critical to seeing his work completed in you. Matthew 12:35-37 talks about the good man bringing good things while the evil man will bring evil, and both will be acquitted or condemned by their words. Let your conversation be full of the word of God because those words draw blessing to you. Proverbs 18:21 warns us of how powerful the tongue is because it can bring life or death, and those who love it will eat of its fruit. What are you going to eat?

Proverbs 6:2 speaks of how we are trapped or snared by the words of our mouth. Proverbs 18:20 states, "From the fruit of their mouth a person's stomach is filled; with the harvest of their lips they are satisfied." Remember Romans 10:8-10 telling us that in your mouth and in your heart is the word of faith. We preach that if you confess with your mouth the Lord Jesus Christ as Savior and believe in your heart, you can be freed from the darkness you are in right now. Confession is made of salvation so that is the word that's our foundation. See how important your words are.

Joshua 1:8 says to "Keep this Book of the Law always on your lips; meditate on it day and night, so that you may be careful to do everything written in it. Then you will be prosperous and successful." This is a plan for success that God gave Joshua. Stick with the plan so that as it says in Psalm 19:14, "May these words of my mouth and this meditation of my heart be pleasing in your sight, Lord, my Rock and my Redeemer." We feed ourselves on the word of God to the point where no corruption shall come out of our mouths. Psalm 141:3 ask God to "Set a guard over my mouth, Lord keep watch over the door of my lips." You get to speak the word of God over yourself and those words will be, according to Philippians 4:8, true, noble, right, pure, lovely, admirable, excellent, or praiseworthy. Ephesians 4:29 admonishes us to let only good words come out of our mouth so we can be helpful to others. By his grace we are overcomers in Revelations 12:11, "They triumphed over him, by the blood of the Lamb, and by the word of their testimony; they did not love their lives so much as to shrink from death."

Mark 11:22-23 tells us to have faith in God with no doubt then ask and believe and things will happen. Sometimes we have to wait, but while we wait, it says in Isaiah 40:31 "but those who hope in the Lord will renew their strength. They will soar on wings like eagles; they will run and not grow weary; they will walk and not be faint." We must learn to trust him and lean up on him wholeheartedly with everything. When you serve the living God with everything that's within you, every moment of every day, with all your heart, mind and soul you can't help but be an overcomer. I'm sharing all these things that you would know the truth and the truth would set you free. I love you and would do anything to help.

To continue to advance your studies, I would advise you to get two or three versions of the Bible and the Strong's Exhaustive Concordance. I enjoy using the New English Standard Bible as it has a dictionary. The Amplified Bible explains verses in depth and has been around a long time. It will help you open your mind up to get a deeper view of a particular verse. For example, Read John 3:16 out of any of the versions and then read it in the amplified to see how helpful it can be. Try to get other major trustworthy versions that you are comfortable reading and understanding. Remember the Holy Spirit will guide you.

As we near the end of this book I want to encourage you to get in church somewhere that believes in Jesus Christ and him crucified. Malachi 3:10 talks about tithing and giving your finances and prioritizing your giving unto the Lord. We know that the Holy Spirit will lead you and guide you into all truth. If there's something you don't understand just put it on the shelf and pray about it, seek the Lord and study it out and the Holy Spirit will guide you . It is important to hang out around Christian people who will encourage you in your walk with the Lord. Let your Bible study and prayer time become a strong foundation. Remember that Jesus is The Refuge so run into his presence every day.

ABOUT THE AUTHOR

Born in Stuttgart, Arkansas and raised in Dewitt, Arkansas. An only child, loved and cared for always. The best mom and dad ever. Attended college in Joplin, Missouri. Met the most beautiful woman in the world. She kissed me under an old oak tree and that was it! Two boys, five grandkids and two great-grandchildren.

Contact: dew_therefuge@yahoo.com

https://www.facebook.com/dewtherefuge/

Made in the USA
Monee, IL
06 August 2024

62786515R00046